Look - Book 3

By Viola & Zaida Stefano

The rights of Viola & Zaida Stefano to be identified as the authors of this work have been asserted by them in accordance with the **Copyright Amendment (Moral Rights) Act 2000.**

All rights reserved. Apart from any use as permitted by the authors & under the **Copyright Act 1968**, no part may be reproduced, copied, scanned, stored in a retrieval system, recorded, or shared, by any means or in any form, without prior written permission from the publisher.

A catalogue record of this book is available from the **National Library of Australia.**

ISBN: 978-0-6458056-6-6

Authors: Viola Stefano & Zaida Stefano
Illustrations, photographs, cover & internal designs: Zaida Stefano

Illustrations copyright © Zaida Stefano 2023
Design copyright © Zaida Stefano 2023
Photographs copyright © Zaida Stefano 2023

Disclaimer: The content presented in this book is meant for educational purposes only. The authors & publisher claim no accountability to any entity or person for any liability, damage, or loss caused or assumed to be caused directly or indirectly as a consequence of the application, use, or interpretation of the material in this book.

VeeZee Publications

Copyright © VeeZee Publications Pty Ltd 2023
First published in Australia in 2023
by VeeZee Publications Pty Ltd
veezeepublications.com

Learning made easy with

VeeZee!

- Focus Core words in 'Look - Book 3' and the 'Look' series
- Secondary Core words in 'Look - Book 3' and the 'Look' series
- Other secondary Core words in the 'Look' series but **NOT** in 'Look - Book 3'

Core Vocabulary used throughout **VeeZee Publications**				
I	want	can	stop	look
like	more	he	go	see
here	what	do	the	and
out	where	we	it	up
not	they	when	that	down
she	now	them	is	put
help	off	you	yes	on
turn	who	this	no	why
done	make	a	to	under
come	in	some	which	there
open	get	good	same	home

All Core word readers through the various series in VeeZee Publications have been developed around specific themes. The themed photos and illustrations present a backdrop for the Core words used in each book. Your students are exploring and interpreting the messages conveyed by these images. They are learning to consider the text in order to understand the images. They are therefore making links between images and the corresponding texts. You are using a range of Core words when discussing the photos and illustrations with your students, especially; who, what, where, when and why. The use of these 'question' words in discussion further reinforces their meanings and their associations with surrounding words. We recommend that students without a vision impairment also explore the readers designed for students with low vision. This will support interaction and discussion amongst the students. It is our hope that this will ultimately promote acceptance, understanding, compassion and teamwork, thus cultivating true inclusion.

We hope you have fun discovering what animals are in our 'Look' books. Not all of our animals have been named, so good luck with your research!

Who in your family likes birds, and why?

Look. I want to look.

2

Look. I want to look here.

4

Look. I want to look there.

I want to look here now.

8

I want to look there now.

10

I want to look at them now.

Mum and dad want to look at them too.

Come look here mum and dad.

Turn back. Come and look at this lion.

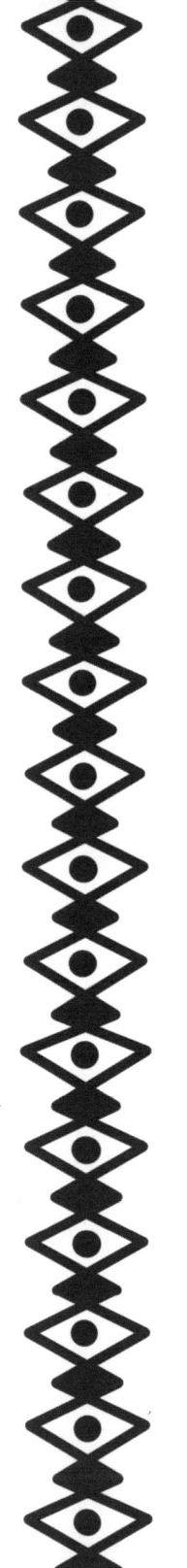

Turn back. Can you look here now?

Look. Turn left. We can look at it.

22

Look. Turn right. We can look at it.

24

Look. I can see some birds.

Look now. I can see more birds.

Come look. We can look at this.

Come look. We can look at that.

32

Words in this book

I	want	we
here	them	more
now	turn	come
to	you	it
mum	this	dad

Words in this book

some	see	and
there	look	can
right	left	at
birds	back	lion
that	too	

Do you know the focus and secondary Core words: 'look', 'I' and 'now'? Read the words along each line.						
I	look	now	look	now	look	I
look	now	look	now	I	look	now
I	look	now	look	now	now	look
look	now	I	now	look	now	I
look	I	look	now	now	look	look
I	look	now	I	look	now	look
now	I	look	now	I	I	look

Do you know the focus and secondary Core words in this book (refer to Core word table)? Find them along each line, point to them and say them. Read the other words too once you have pointed to the Core words.

that	look	want	can	here	mum	at
right	back	more	we	it	see	and
now	this	some	to	look	I	left
turn	look	them	there	see	here	at
come	you	want	lion	to	and	more
them	this	too	right	look	now	back
you	come	look	turn	dad	we	birds

How many times did you read the word 'look'?

Make new words with '__ack', e.g., 'black'. Write sentences using these words.

We hope you had fun reading!

VeeZee Publications

Wait, there's more!

Visit our website for information about our range of readers & supporting products.

veezeepublications.com

www.ingramcontent.com/pod-product-compliance
Lightning Source LLC
Chambersburg PA
CBHW050853010526
44107CB00047BA/1594